Manifesting – Beginners Guide

Manifestation Strategies to Achieve Your Desires for Money, Love, Abundance, Happiness, and Success to Become Your Greatest Self

Olivia Clifford

© **Copyright 2021 - All rights reserved.**

The content contained within this book may not be reproduced, duplicated or transmitted without direct written permission from the author or the publisher.

Under no circumstances will any blame or legal responsibility be held against the publisher, or author, for any damages, reparation, or monetary loss due to the information contained within this book, either directly or indirectly.

Legal Notice:

This book is copyright protected. It is only for personal use. You cannot amend, distribute, sell, use, quote or paraphrase any part, or the content within this book, without the consent of the author or publisher.

Disclaimer Notice:

Please note the information contained within this document is for educational and entertainment purposes only. All effort has been executed to present accurate, up to date, reliable, complete information. No warranties of any kind are declared or implied. Readers acknowledge that the author is not engaged in the rendering of legal, financial, medical or professional advice. The content within this book has been derived from various sources. Please consult a licensed professional before attempting any techniques outlined in this book.

By reading this document, the reader agrees that under no circumstances is the author responsible for any losses, direct or indirect, that are incurred as a result of the use of the information contained within this document, including, but not limited to, errors, omissions, or inaccuracies.

Table of Contents

Table of Contents

Introduction

Chapter 1: The Law of Attraction

Chapter 2: The Power of Now

Chapter 3: Moving Into Alignment and Staying There

Chapter 4: Get Out of Your Own Way – Overcome Self-Sabotage

Chapter 5: The Secret Behind Manifesting

Chapter 6: Live Life Fully

Final Thoughts

References

Introduction

Lao Tzu once asserted that "A journey of a thousand miles begins with a single step" (Literary Devices, 2019). There is some immense truth to this statement as we look toward achieving what we want in life. Undeniably, there is a lot that we demand in life. In fact, true happiness, love, abundance, and all our heart's desires are governed by the achievements we make. How great can life be if only you had faith in the first step you take. To get to your destination, you don't have to worry about how you will get there. Rather, you only need to believe in yourself and take the first step. This is what the power of manifesting is all about - Faith in the unseen.

When you stop to reflect on your life and the things you desire for yourself, chances are you fill your mind and heart with worry and anxiety. We often stress ourselves because we think that our goals are too far-fetched. Worse, we even believe that we are walking down the wrong path in life. But the truth of the matter is that the universe always delivers. The universe always gifts us with what we want if only we ask in the right manner. The phrase, "Ask and it will be given to you; seek and you will find; knock, and the door will be opened to you,", is not new to most of us (Bible Hub, 2021). We're always hopeful for tomorrow because we believe that we would achieve something we had planned. So, why is it so difficult to believe that you can manifest what you want into your life?

Maybe you're thinking of manifesting abundance, money, wealth, love, fruitful relationships, and a great career. It doesn't matter what you want to manifest; the most important thing is for you to believe with conviction that it's possible. Manifesting – Beginners Guide will reveal what you need to do to start practicing how to attract what you want into your life. It's a well-known fact that you're what you think about most of the time. Consequently, by aligning your thoughts to the things you desire, there is no doubt that, sooner or later, you will live your best life.

That said, one of the main keys that will guarantee you manifest what you want into your life is - the law of attraction. This is one of the laws of the universe that will guide you in bringing what you want into your life. It's a simple law that will shape your life in ways you never imagined before. All you have to do is to determine what you want in life and go for it.

Think about living the life of your dreams. Keep in mind that one of the most crucial things you need to work on as you use this guide to learn more about manifesting strategies is your belief system. There is nothing that is beyond your reach if you truly believe in yourself. That's how the universe works. When great things start manifesting into your life, you will be amazed as the universe's energies work life's magic. So, ask in the right way, seek in the right direction, and knock on the right doors. When this happens, you will live a life full of abundance and joy.

Start developing an abundance mindset as you read this book. Take a moment to connect with your higher self. Allow positive, fulfilling thoughts to fill your mind. There is nothing you lack in this world. You are enough, and that you have enough. Take a look around you and express gratitude for the things you already have. Life didn't just happen by chance. You deserve what you have, and you have the ability to attract more into your life. Be confident in yourself and the path you're about to take into a whole new world full of abundance.

Before we begin, have it in mind that manifesting what you want in life isn't about asking the universe and expecting things to happen. You need to take a bold step and take action on your goals and dreams. Action is what is required from you. It's vital that you surround yourself with energies that are in line with what you want. Manifesting isn't a passive exercise. Fortunately, once you develop the right habits that attract what you want in life, everything else will fall into place. So, don't be discouraged.

Let's begin!

Chapter 1: The Law of Attraction

Just like the law of gravity, the law of attraction is always in action. Believe it or not, one of the main keys to manifesting what you want in life is by understanding that there is energy in you. It's essential to cultivate the energy within you to attract what you want in life. You've often heard that you create the life you want. Well, this is true. You're always creating the reality that you call life every day. This happens through your thoughts, whether consciously or subconsciously.

The law of attraction applies to your life in many ways. Change your thoughts for a moment, and you will be happy or sad, depending on the direction of your thoughts. For instance, think of an experience that changed your life in the past. When you immerse yourself in the positive thought, chances are you will find yourself smiling. Now, think of a painful experience that you rarely want to be associated with. There is nothing worth smiling about with such negative thoughts. Consequently, you might feel weary just at the thought of it. What this means is that you can change how you feel by simply changing your thoughts. This is how you create reality in your everyday life.

In the same way, you can start manifesting what you want into your life by leveraging the law of attraction. This law will change your life by the simple fact that you will be more conscious of how and what you think about most of the time. In other words, you will be more in control of your life.

One amazing thing about the law of attraction is that it will introduce you to a world full of miracles. It gives you an opportunity to see past the impossibilities that might have been holding you back. Once you master this law, it would be easy for you to challenge the scarcity mindset that often deters people from succeeding and achieving their goals.

What Is the Law of Attraction?

Put it simply, the law of attraction indicates that you attract the life you want by focusing on the things you would want in your life. This can also be understood in the form of - energy flows where attention goes. With this in mind, the most important thing you need to focus on is to determine what you want in life. Ask yourself - "What do I really want?" This is an important question that would ensure you know where to focus your energy. Ideally, this is what intentional living is all about.

Strive to focus on the positive things in life, and good things will manifest in your path. Make a list of the things you would wish to accomplish. Create positive affirmations around your goals. Suppose you continuously affirm to yourself that you're great or that you're wealthy and blessed. In that case, the universe will sync with your positive energies.

On the contrary, if you focus on things you lack, this will only evoke negative emotions. When this happens, negativity will haunt you like a plague. Ever wondered why a series of bad events might happen in your life when you focus on how life is not working out for you? Well, this is one way in which the law of attraction works.

When you're feeling enthusiastic, excited, happy, and appreciative of how life is good to you, you send out positive vibes. Interestingly, good things will continue manifesting in your path. This means that you can learn and master how to leverage the law of attraction at all times. Of course, this is not easy, especially when you're going through a difficult time. But the law of attraction works like magic. Your life can quickly transform right before your eyes, and you would be surprised with how life happens for you.

The following are three fundamental tenets of the law of attraction.

You Are the Creator

The law of attraction is based on the simple principle that life doesn't just happen. You're the creator of the reality that manifests in your life. No one but you is responsible for your life. You have control over the experiences that you go through in life. The people you interact with, the friends you have, the amount of money you get, your level of happiness, etc. It sounds crazy, but it's true. Understanding the power you have over your life comes with the revelation that you're not a victim in life. Rather, life happens for you - just as you want it. Amazing, right?

When you finally understand how the law of attraction works, you enter into a realm where you use your mind to shape your life. A change of thought is all you need to start looking at challenges from a positive perspective. What's more, you will begin to live abundantly because you know there is power within you to change your life without allowing self-limiting doubts to get the best of you. Therefore, you're always creating your life. Nothing should stop you from creating a life you fancy. Just take the first step, as Lao Tzu mentioned in his quote regarding taking the first step in your journey of a thousand miles.

Still skeptical about how you can attract what you want into your life? Well, let's consider how you can use the law of attraction to manifest money.

Given the opportunity, we all would want to live abundantly by accumulating more wealth. But one of the biggest challenges most people face is that they have a poor relationship with money. This prevents them from fully accomplishing their goals and living the life they've always wanted. Manifesting money starts in the mind. Most individuals find it challenging to think positively about money because of their negative belief system.

The law of attraction comes in to help you change your belief system. This is what you need to start thinking of prosperity and amassing the wealth you need into your life. However, for this to work, you must take action and put the law into practice.

Start identifying some of the limiting beliefs you have about money. For instance, growing up, we were made to believe that money is the root of all evil or that money doesn't grow on trees, or money can't buy you happiness. These are examples of limiting beliefs that influence you to think negatively about money. It's crucial to see money as a tool that will help you make your dreams a reality. More importantly, money is accessible, and it's available in unlimited supply. With this mentality, it's easier for you to work toward manifesting wealth in your life.

The law of attraction also works through the power of visualization. Whatever you're thinking of acquiring into your life, you need to think like you already have it. For instance, visualize having enough money that you don't have to go from paycheck to paycheck trying to make ends meet. Think of financial freedom and how it can give you an opportunity to follow your passion without the need to get paid for it. Once you develop this picture in your mind, act like it. Act like you already have the amount of money you need. How would your life change? Live like you're wealthy, and the universe will listen to you through your thoughts and emotions. The point here is that visualization helps to create an abundance mindset. And everything else works like magic to ensure you live a fulfilling life.

Thoughts Become Things

The law of attraction is also based on the principle that your thoughts act as magnets. Basically, you are what you think about, which means that you can change your life by changing your thoughts. The idea here is that you should raise your awareness of your thoughts. If you're constantly thinking of good things, you increase the chances of great things happening in your life. The best part is that you can easily shift your thoughts even when you're not thinking positively. By making conscious efforts to take control of your thoughts, you also evoke positive vibes that attract good things your way.

You Attract What You Give Attention To

Like attracts like. And in the same, the energy goes where the attention flows. It's that simple. The law of attraction indicates that you attract everything that you pay attention to. The worst mistake we often make in life is that we tend to focus more on the things we don't want. The problem with this style of thinking is that we attract negativity. So, people who often dread going broke will find themselves struggling with their finances. The same case applies to relationships and other facets of your life.

When putting the law of attraction into practice, consider asking the universe for what you want. Stop thinking about what you don't want. If you're going to succeed in your career, focus more on what it takes for you to succeed. Strive to live intentionally. By doing this, you will start living a fulfilling life. Things will fall into place, not because you're working extra hard, but because your energies are in line with what you want.

With regards to your relationships, if you're looking to create a life full of love, focus on exuding love to the people around you. Be the love that you wish to attract. Put yourself first and practice self-love. Take care of yourself so you can be in a better position to help those around you. Learn to express gratitude for the fruitful relationships you share with others. This is how you create a sense of abundance around you.

The law of attraction is easy to think about but difficult to implement. Why? Because people allow themselves to fall prey to negative bias. Human beings are hardwired to think negatively. This means that it's easy for you to think of the worst that might happen to you compared to thinking of greatness and abundance. Leverage the power vested in you to attract the life you want. You don't have to wait any longer to start manifesting love, bliss, money, abundance, and success into your life. Start taking small baby steps in the right direction. This can be as simple as changing your thoughts.

Chapter 2: The Power of Now

There is no reason to think that life can be free from pain and sorrow. The best thing you can do to overcome challenges in your path is to learn to live with them. And the worst thing you should think of doing is to try and avoid them. Doing this will only cause you more pain and sorrow. Why? Because you will fight a losing battle, and that's where life seems unbearable.

However, most of the pains and sorrow we experience are self-inflicted. Usually, this happens when we allow our minds to run our lives. The pain most people go through comes in the form of nonacceptance or some sort of resistance to how life has transitioned. Perhaps you might be too judgmental to appreciate the importance of change in your life. When this happens, negativity creeps in, and you would conclude that life is not fair. The mind always strives to escape from the present moment. The more you associate with your mind, the more likely you will suffer. On the contrary, if you can accept to live in the NOW, you can easily free yourself from pain and your egoic mind.

The mind always seeks to run the show. We should understand here that when the mind is in control, you will rarely live in the present moment. You will find yourself either living in the past or the future. In other words, your true nature becomes shadowed by the mind. To separate yourself from the mind, you should realize that you only have NOW to change and live a happy and blissful life. This means saying 'yes' to the present moment at all times. Why try to oppose the flow of life and expect to be happy? Just say 'yes' to life, and you will be amazed at how life will work for you and not against you.

If you stopped for a moment and gave it a thought, NOW is all you have got in life. You can effortlessly manifest what you want by choosing to accept how life is and how it works. The past is the past. You have no control over it. The same case applies to the future. We often waste time and energy living in the past and worrying too much about the uncertain future. This should change. Acknowledge that life will only work for you when you accept what you can't change and take action on what you can change.

The law of attraction also delves around living in the now and enjoying every moment of it. Most people go through life saying that they will be happy when certain things happen. We often find ourselves saying, "I will be happy when I get money," or "I will be happy when I find my soulmate." The problem with this attitude is that you never stop to enjoy the present moment. You're focused on the future while doing your best to resist the reality of NOW. At the end of the day, you deprive yourself of true happiness and bliss found in enjoying what life has offered you.

Of course, it's good to anticipate good things in your life. However, we should not expect too much to the point where we are dissatisfied with our current lives. So, as you shift your thoughts to think positively and visualize an amazing future, always ensure that you stay in the present moment.

A Word About Desire

We are all creatures of desire. Most of our lives are bound by the desires we have. We desire better lives, happy relationships, more money, joy, and so on. From a spiritual perspective, finding peace is also a desire we often aspire. While we have little control over our wishes, the biggest problem we create for ourselves is attaching ourselves to these desires.

There are different ways of living in the NOW. You might choose to live in joy or misery. Living in misery puts your life on hold and prevents you from manifesting what you want into your life. Conversely, living in joy allows you to enjoy the flow of life and the blessings that come with it.

To attract what you want into your life, you should realize that we consciously and unconsciously send out our desires to the universe.

Similarly, we should strive to fully engage in the present moment. To put the law of attraction and the power of now together, it's vital that you excitedly anticipate a great future while doing your best to love how you're currently living.

War on Fear

When you think about the life you would want to live, fear quickly creeps in and stops you from believing that you can ever enjoy life. Say you're thinking of manifesting more money into your life. Fear will drive you to think of your current financial situation. Perhaps there is a lot you need to handle before you can think of financial freedom. You may also think of the boring career you have and how challenging it is to earn and save money. These are frightening thoughts. Fear prevents us from taking action on our goals.

However, fear is part of life. In some cases, fear is good as it prevents us from doing things that would have caused us pain. For instance, if you weren't afraid of fire, you may risk putting your hand in a fire. But fear is not the main reason why you can't put your hand in a fire. Instead, it's because you're aware that you can get burned. Intelligence and common sense ensure that you don't need to fear to stay away from unnecessary danger.

The fears we often face come in different forms: worry, unease, dread, tension, anxiety, nervousness, and so on. This type of fear is different because it's based on something that might happen. Therefore, while you're doing your best to stay in the present moment, the mind is busy wandering in the future. If you identify yourself with your mind, it means that you will continuously live in fear. Ego will run your life.

Naturally, your ego is always insecure and vulnerable. It perceives itself as constantly in danger. The mind responds through emotions, and the message the body receives from your ego is the false state of mind. You may feel like you're under threat because of the false state of mind. The body responds by generating unnecessary fear.

Acceptance is one effective way of dealing with your fears. What this means is that you should not try to avoid fearful thoughts. Life is full of challenges, and there is nothing you can do about it. Instead of escaping your fears, welcome them and find a way of dealing with them. What you resist will persist. Relax into the present moment by using meditation and breathing exercises. This will liberate you from the false state of the mind that might prevent you from being happy.

Another effective way of dealing with your fears is by learning to appreciate life as it is and expressing gratitude. By expressing gratitude, you allow yourself to focus more on the gifts the universe has bestowed into your life. You will want to focus more on the good side of life. Make a list of the things you're grateful for. This is an exercise you should do every day. A habit of expressing gratitude will also help you see the good even in bad situations. With the positive mindset that you would have developed, you will focus more on learning from the difficult times you face in life. After all, you can't go through life without experiencing challenges. So, it's best that you learn from them and work toward becoming the best version of yourself.

To manifest what you want into your life, strive to change your narrative. Stop focusing on the things you don't want. Sure, fear will drive you to think of the worst that might happen. But when you disassociate yourself from your mind, you will realize that the mind is only creating a false state to prevent you from doing something. Accordingly, you will live in the NOW and focus more on what you really want.

More importantly, retrain your brain to think in the direction that you're heading. The mind has a mind of its own. If you can't control your mind, it will use you. Try not to quickly label situations or people as either right or wrong, good or bad. We all live separate lives with different destinies. The lessons you learn in life might differ from what others learn. And, that's okay. Give people the permission to live their lives without bringing yourself unnecessary pain.

Changing your habits is a process. You can't become the person you want to be overnight. Think of yourself as a work in progress. This means taking the time to improve your life every day. You will be going through a major transition if only you focus on doing the things that bring you an inch closer to your dreams and goals. You should understand that it's okay to be uncomfortable. Things might not work out immediately for you but focus on appreciating your life as it is. Remember, it's a topsy-turvy journey, and there is nothing you can do about it but to adjust and live intentionally. So, get comfortable being uncomfortable.

Chapter 3: Moving Into Alignment and Staying There

When you have identified what you need in life, you need to be in alignment with what you want. Again, this is closely related to what the law of attraction articulates. It's crucial that you are an energetic match with what you want to manifest into your life. This form of alignment requires that you feel good about having or getting whatever it is you wanted. So, instead of being worried or stressed, you should be happy and relaxed with a strong conviction that you will get what you want. This chapter will help you understand how you can move into alignment and stay there without getting distracted.

The idea of aligning yourself with desires implies that you free yourself from the excessive need around that which you strongly desire. It means that you're open to your desires manifesting in varying ways. Moreover, it also means that you're not burdened by how things have to happen. This is because you can't control how things should manifest in your life. Rather, you should be prepared for anything that comes your way and welcome it wholeheartedly.

Theoretically, aligning yourself might sound easy, but in practice, it's not that straightforward. Your natural resistance to change might show up and prevent you from truly believing that everything will fall into place.

It's also worth noting that there are good moments when you feel like things are finally working out. In most cases, these moments don't last for long. We often have those times when we feel motivated to do something. And it is during these times that we feel driven toward our goals. However, this motivation quickly fades away when we face challenges. It's life, right? We tend to live reactively, allowing our beliefs and moods to be affected by the experiences we go through.

Life is not all about achieving a perfect state to manifest what we want. However, it's vital that we focus on uplifting our spirits rather than feeling bad most of the time. In other words, we need to be in alignment instead of being out of it.

Building the right momentum toward aligning yourself in the right way shouldn't be difficult. Your best approach should be to simplify the whole process. This means raising your awareness of your beliefs, thoughts, and feelings that will ensure you attract what you want and weaken the energies that might stop you from reaching your goals.

Determining Your Reasons 'Why'

Attracting what you want in life revolves around 'what' you want. What do you want to manifest now that you're reading this book? Is it love, money, happiness, wealth, abundance? Of course, we all have different desires. Which means your desires will differ from someone else's. The most important thing is to understand that we all have unique paths. So, determining what you really want is a personal approach to knowing what brings you happiness and zeal into your life.

Determining 'what' you want will be the first step that subsequently makes you focus on the 'how.' Before you think about 'how' you will get money, the first step is to determine whether it's money you truly want in your life.

Trusting that everything will work out sounds awesome, and there is no doubt that we all yearn to do the necessary to manifest what we want. However, the mind stops us from fully trusting and believing that we will get what we want. This is one of the main stumbling blocks that deter us from building the momentum we need to manifest. Additionally, another element that might also mess with our quest is our unhealthy attachment with the 'what.' Most people are overly attached to the idea of getting money simply because they think that money will make them happy or that it will change their lives completely. At the end of the day, when this fails to happen, they give up and develop negative attitudes toward money and the overall idea of working hard toward it.

Unconsciously, we normally turn the 'what' into 'how.' We tend to think that whatever we want has to happen so that we can manifest what we want. The reality is that sometimes that which we want might not represent what we truly want. And that's okay. Whatever you're thinking of manifesting is just a fraction of how life can be amazing.

You need to take a step back and understand the reasons behind that which you want. The more you cognize, the deeper reasons why it is easier for you to detach yourself from your desires. More importantly, this also makes it easy for you to align yourself with the energies tied to the desired outcomes NOW. And the best thing is that it doesn't matter what your current situation looks like. It's possible to feel good in the present moment knowing that you've already achieved what you want.

So, why do you want to manifest the desires you have in mind? This is not a simple, Yes or No question. To garner a deeper understanding of why you want something, you need to dig deeper and connect with your emotions. For instance, maybe you want to find love because you're ready to settle down and have a family. Or you want more money to ensure you're happy and less stressed meeting your financial obligations. Think about the reasons behind your quest. Why is it important to you to manifest these things? What makes you think that getting that thing will bring fulfillment into your life? You need to keep asking yourself these questions until you can't go deeper. At this point, you would have reached the core reasons why you need to manifest certain things into your life.

Remember, when determining your reasons why as it's vital that you dwell on the positive. Focus less on what you don't want. The law of attraction requires that you pay attention to what you want and not what you don't want. So, keep your eyes on the prize.

The essence of knowing your 'whys' ensures that you go beyond the feeling tied to what you want. It also helps in bringing clarity into your desires. When you're clear and honest with yourself about what you really want, you will go with the flow of life. Life becomes simple. You will want to live intentionally and purposefully because you know what you want and how to get there. Everything else becomes nothing but a distraction, and you will want to get rid of all these stumbling blocks in your way.

The Universe Will Always Deliver

Let's be honest for a moment here; there is no doubt that we rarely believe that we can actually get what we want. You've been through different relationships, and you can't stop to believe that you can settle down and have a wonderful family. Maybe you're bankrupt, and the last thing you can think about is your life changing and amassing wealth. Admittedly, it sounds like a different world where we are not meant to reside. It's like a fantasy, and our dreams are nothing but mere dreams that will never come true.

Arguably, we all have certain beliefs that we find it daunting to shift or deviate from them. At times, we are too attached to the outcomes of what we want, and we can't think of anything else that might make us happier. We also judge our lives based on our circumstances and our emotional state. The past is also something that we use to gauge whether things will be okay. When things are not turning out as expected, we justify why this might be happening. Interestingly, we have all the reasons to console ourselves that we're just not lucky enough.

With everything going on inside our minds, we are certain that we shouldn't be thinking negatively about ourselves. But we can't help it because it's just how things are unfolding themselves. The problem is that there is so much negative energy around our lives, and we can't see past the challenges we might be facing.

Unfortunately, our negative attitudes don't align us with what we want. Instead, we stray away from this alignment, and things get worse. We worry too much that our dreams will never come true. We also worry that we've messed up everything and that life will not change as we desire.

The beauty of life is that you don't have to master taking control of your emotions or eliminating self-limiting beliefs completely for you to attract what you want. You don't have to perfect your life. Negative emotions surrounding your life will always be there. The same case applies to the self-limiting beliefs that hold you back. It's the nature of life, and there is a lot we need to do to continuously think positively and attract what we want.

You can change your narrative by just being receptive to the universe, even if you don't know how it will happen. Even believing for a few minutes that it's possible can make a huge difference. The more you enter that space where you trust, believe, and receive what you want, the more likely you will manifest your desires. You need to trust that everything will be okay without worrying about what you have no control over. Amazing things will happen in your life because the universe always delivers. All you need to do is to believe that it's possible.

Strengthen your faith and appreciate the fact that there are things happening behind the scenes to streamline your life. Sure, you don't know what is happening, but deep inside, you trust that something good will show up. You don't need to understand the 'how'; the 'how' will take care of itself.

In those beautiful moments of believing and trusting that the universe will deliver, positive energy of manifestation will fill your space. You will start living in the NOW with less worry about the future. You will also be more receptive to the things happening in your life. When you get to this point, the power of manifestation will transform your life forever.

Dealing With Conflicting Energies

Over time, good things will start happening in your life. Your relationships may get better, and you may start seeing the light at the end of the tunnel in your finances. These are great signs that you're on the right path. Trust builds, and your belief system will start to shift. You will also have a positive attitude toward everything going on.

However, you should realize that it won't be a smooth sail all the way. Energies that were once holding you back will keep resurfacing. And the worst thing is that, at times, you won't notice their effects on your mission.

Somewhere along the way, you may find yourself worrying that you did something wrong. You could feel like you've messed up and erased all the progress you've made. Negativity will build-up, and if you fail to take action, you might fall back to where you started. When this happens, it's crucial to remind yourself that there is nothing wrong going on. Challenges are part of the process, so it's best that you learn how to welcome them. We all have our low moments in life, even when everything is going smoothly. The best thing we can do to lift our spirits is to understand that life will never be smooth. There are ups and downs that we have to face, and it's during our weak moments that we leverage our strengths to see past difficulties.

In those trying moments, strive to understand what the experience might be teaching you. Don't avoid negative feelings. Connect with them and find out what life might be teaching you. Go with the flow. Eventually, you will realize that there is some energy worked to change your life in one way or another. After all, what doesn't kill you will make you stronger.

Generally, life would have been more exciting if you could just believe in something, and it manifests right away. Well, sometimes it's this easy, but on rare occasions. Most of the time, we have to deal with the resistance that comes from within. You want something, but your mind thinks the other way. Worse, it might give you all sorts of reasons not to believe that you can manifest what you want into your life. But there is hope as things get better with time. With time, you will find it easier to move into a space where you believe and trust that the universe will deliver. When unfortunate events occur, you won't be surprised or overwhelmed. You will be more accepting of these circumstances, and that you will strive to shift your attention to what you want.

Aligning yourself with your manifestations won't be easy at first. Your human, and all along, you've shaped your beliefs and attitudes based on your past. It will take some time to change this. Be patient as you go through this transition. Remember to celebrate the manifestations that give you a reason to believe that you're on the right path. The little positive energy that radiates within you can snowball gradually.

Chapter 4: Get Out of Your Own Way - Overcome Self-Sabotage

To most people, self-sabotage is a defense mechanism. When good things fail to manifest in your life, you have all the excuses you need to change direction and walk a different path. Often, we allow our brains to control us. Unconsciously, we find ourselves holding on to failure, loss, rejection, and fear. This prevents us from staying motivated toward the big goals that we have set for ourselves. Perhaps you thought of starting a business or changing careers. The thought that you might fail in the process can quickly derail your progress.

Fortunately, you can get out of your own way and overcome self-sabotage behaviors. The worst thing about self-sabotage is that it creates unnecessary pain in our lives. Fear, failure, doubt, rejection, and so on can make you feel like you're not living your best life. At some point, you may start doubting yourself, wondering whether there is something that you're not doing to succeed.

Self-sabotage behavior can take different forms. For some, it can take the form of avoidance or procrastination. For others, it might look like relieving stress in unhealthy ways, like wasting money, overeating, or abusing alcohol or drugs. To manifest what you want in your life, it's vital that you learn how to overcome such behaviors.

Why Do We Self-Sabotage Our Efforts?

It's a common thing to find people feeling anxious and stressed when trying to accomplish certain goals. When the worst happens, they get angry with themselves and feel discouraged in the process. The negative feelings they experience prevent them from doing what they need to do to thrive. Basically, these are signs of self-sabotage.

The moment you doubt yourself, your self-esteem and self-confidence is eroded. Now, with every subsequent failure you experience in trying to accomplish your goal, you affirm to yourself that indeed you're a failure or that you can't achieve something. In other words, destructive behavior undermines your efforts. You may not notice it at first, but when such behaviors become a habit, they develop into psychological self-harm.

We tend to self-sabotage because of our low self-esteem. The cause can vary from one person to another, but the effects are similar: Believing that you're not worthy of success, joy, and happiness, or feelings of worthlessness, and even escalating to self-hatred.

You may be troubled that your failure might mean that your friends and family will think less of you. You may also think that your success might make your colleagues jealous of you. These negative feelings and thoughts often lead to negative self-talk. This further fuels the fears and beliefs you've developed over time.

Most individuals self-sabotage as a way of taking control of the situation they might be facing. It gives them a reason to think that they are taking control of the situation. For instance, by procrastinating things, you give yourself a short-term boost in your confidence that you can accomplish something. But ultimately, such behaviors are destructive.

In line with the notion of manifesting what you want in life, self-sabotage can hold you back. You may have set goals and decided to commit yourself to a particular mission. Unconsciously, your mind might stop you from taking action on what you think is important. For instance, if you're trying to manifest love, self-sabotage will make you ignore potential partners. If you're thinking of finding yourself a new job, self-sabotage will drive you to procrastinate the need to fine-tune your resume.

Of course, it's natural to get disheartened or frustrated when you fail to manifest what you want. But it's important to remember that you're not alone. This happens to everyone. The best thing you can do is maintain a positive attitude toward what you really want. If you're not manifesting what you want, patience and hard work will take you all the way. The universe will never fail you.

Overcoming Self-Defeating Behavior

To stop self-sabotaging yourself, you need to shift your mindset. Instead of allowing negative thoughts to fill your mind, you should consider shifting your thoughts. It is through a positive mindset that you are better placed to manifest what you truly want. The following pointers should help you get started.

Uncover Self-Destructive Behavior

Start by digging the reasons behind your self-sabotaging behavior. What is that thing that is holding you back? What's stopping you from believing that you can accomplish your goals? Your reasons are tied to the desires you have in mind. For example, if you're looking to manifest abundance, self-sabotage will drive you to think of all the reasons why this can't happen for you. Strive to understand what the other side of you believes. Why does your mind trick you into believing that you can't attract abundance your way?

Determine the reasons behind your destructive behaviors. Make a list of these things. In terms of abundance, for example, your subconscious mind might think that there is a lot you lack for you to live a fulfilled life. Maybe you're not happy in your relationship or that your businesses are not paying off. Perhaps you've developed a habit of abusing alcohol.

Armed with a list of the reasons why you might not be doing something, challenge yourself to go against your subconscious mind. Do something you initially told yourself you couldn't manage. Face your fears and take control of your mind.

Recognize Self-Sabotaging Habits

Now, once you've identified some of the destructive behaviors holding you back, the next step is to develop new productive habits. It takes time to develop a habit. So, you need to be patient to make changes in your life that will stick. Some common destructive habits that you will have to work on include procrastination, perfectionism, and negative self-talk.

Make Significant Changes to Your Life

In addition to replacing old habits with new healthier ones, you should consider making more significant changes. Particularly, find a way of reframing your mindset. Do your best to develop a positive attitude every day. Affirmations can help you start the day on a positive note. Raise your awareness of your self-talk and aim to make this positive. Every time you catch yourself thinking negatively about yourself, reaffirm to yourself that you can become better. You're a work in progress; keep focusing on improving yourself one day at a time.

Creating a vision board is also a great way of developing a positive mindset around the things you wish to manifest. With this vision board, you can paint how you would want your future to look. Through the power of visualization, you can start shifting your mindset to start believing that it's possible to attract what you want. Ensure you notice the small achievements you make along the way as they draw the right energies that bring you in alignment with your manifestations.

Take Time to Self-Reflect

Knowing that you're making progress in life is fulfilling. Consequently, while taking time to change your destructive behaviors, you need to find time to self-reflect. Monitor whether you're developing productive habits that guarantee you don't just live but also thrive. Similarly, notice when certain behaviors stop you from thinking positively and find out why. An ideal way of monitoring your progress is by journaling regularly. Write down your experiences, and you will find it easy to know what works and what doesn't. This way, you can make the necessary changes to improve.

Connect With Your Inner Positive Voice

An integral part of dealing with self-sabotage requires that you silence your inner critic. This is the small voice inside you that continuously reminds you that you can't achieve something. You can be great. In fact, you were born to be great. Therefore, it's important not to allow your inner critic to get the best of you. Stop the negative self-talk inside you and replace this voice with a more rewarding, positive self-talk. You can do this with the help of meditation. Thought-stopping exercises will give you power over your thoughts. As a result, you will learn how to silence the inner chatter in your mind and find the peace you need. The mind can also be exercised like any other muscle. The more you exercise it, the stronger it gets. So, focus on training your brain to think positively.

Chapter 5: The Secret Behind Manifesting

It might take some time to manifest what you want in life. When this happens, it's normal to find yourself wondering whether there is something you should be doing to notice positive changes in your path. If you're not careful, you might even choose to give up altogether, thinking that the power of manifesting doesn't work for you. But you should understand that you're not going through such a dilemma on your own. There are thousands of other people struggling to make the power of manifesting work for them. In fact, most people have tried to apply the law of attraction, but they haven't been successful. Indeed, it's disappointing when you've been spending all your precious time visualizing your ideal life, but nothing works.

So, here we unveil for you the secret that you should apply to make manifesting work for you.

Ask, Believe, Receive

The secret behind manifesting what you want in life is based on the phrase, 'ask, believe, receive.' Chances are that you've decided to read this book because your manifestations are not materializing. This means that you're still searching for that one secret that will change your life forever.

As you look to understand how to apply this secret, it's important to understand that it's not your fault you're not manifesting anything in your life. It could be that you've been misinformed all along about how to manifest your dream life.

When you think of the phrase, 'ask, believe, receive,' it sounds simple. But it's not as straightforward as you might be thinking. The first step is asking. Of course, this might be the easiest thing to do. We all have an idea of what we want in life. So, making your requests to the universe shouldn't be that of a problem. The last step is receiving. Again, this is also not a difficult thing to do because you simply need to welcome positive changes into your life.

Now, the biggest challenge we face is the believing part. This is where most people trip. Believing is not easy because you need to have faith in the unseen for you to manifest what you want. Say you want to manifest wealth. Since you haven't manifested it and you haven't seen it, it becomes daunting to even think that it's possible.

To most people, they believe in the idea that seeing is believing. This means that you will only believe in something when you finally see it with your own eyes. But this contradicts the whole idea of attracting the life you want. For you to receive (and see), you must take a bold step and believe.

Believing in the Unseen

So, how do you start believing in the unseen? Rather than lazing around expecting money to fall in your laps, it's easier for you to find proof that the strategy you're applying works. Think of it this way; you've learned to believe that your trustworthy friend will come through and help you when you need them most. Often, you can't think of the worst because there is some certainty that they will help out. In the same way, you can start believing that the law of attraction will be there to save you when you need help. It doesn't matter what you desire. By making this law your best friend, you bring clarity and certainty into your life. To you, nothing will seem impossible.

It's vital to open your eyes to the cues from the universe that the law of attraction works. Notice the small positive changes in your life and acknowledge them. The more you see and connect with evidence that the law works, the more you strengthen your belief system. Over time, you will learn to trust the universe to deliver.

Take Action

Identify your heart's desires and focus your energies there. While doing this, strive to be deliberate with your actions. You don't have to postpone your happiness into a space that is nonexistent in the present moment. Quit saying that you will be happy and content when this and that happens. Live in the NOW. Act as if you have what you desire. Live like you already have what you want to manifest. If it's money you're looking to manifest, start acting like you're rich. Stop living like you lack something. Live abundantly, and you will align yourself with the right energies to attract what you want.

Be Autonomous

The beauty of manifestation is that everything is yours to decide. This means that you should leverage the power of choice to create the life you desire. Identify what you want in life and decide to live intentionally. This demands that you find clarity in what you want and going for it by taking action. The most important thing to remember is that you should be bold when asking the universe. This means you shouldn't settle for anything less. A strong belief system is what you need to see with conviction that you already have that which you strongly desire.

Chapter 6: Live Life Fully

It's never too late to start living again. Perhaps you're thinking that there is a lot that you need to do for you to start enjoying life once again. But the truth is that you were born to live an adventure. Maybe life has not been easy for you, and you've been stressing over it. Guess what? That's life. You were born to counter these challenges, the hardships, and the pains that come with them. At the end of it all, it is the joy of accomplishing something and overcoming the adversities.

Most people coast through life feeling empty and depressed. If you look around you, you will notice there are people who are just there to pass the time. To put it more specifically, they show no signs of living. Rarely will you find these people showing some excitement about how life is and the new day they are gifted. Interestingly, they cling to memories of what life used to mean to them. But deep down, they long to live life once again. It's sad!

The first step to living your life more fully is accepting one scary fact: You become alive again by welcoming pain. Life is a struggle. That's a fact. So, to experience life, you must understand that pain is integral to keep you alive. You experience joy when you overcome the hardships of life. You build your muscles when you stretch beyond the normal limits. Courage is also built in the face of danger. So, you must get comfortable being uncomfortable.

When you choose to live a comfortable life, you will get bored sooner or later. Why? Because there is nothing challenging about it. There is no reason to enjoy the thrill of accomplishing something that you've been working hard to bring into your life. Therefore, give up the idea of living a comfortable life. Life is all about pressing on. You may not have achieved your dreams, but keep pressing on. Expect the best to happen by trusting your good friend, the law of attraction. The universe will not disappoint you.

Take a look at the most successful people you often admire; these people stand out because they take risks and embrace failure in everything they do. They learn from their failures, and they choose never to get comfortable. Well, now that you know the secret path to this life, you can also live the life of your dreams, if you want.

To this point, you know what you want in life. But the question is, are you ready to pay the price. Living your life more fully comes with a hefty price tag. It's easy to assume that you will change your life by following a specific strategy or that you will live a happy and content life. However, the most challenging decision you need to make is to decide to live. This means accepting the fact that pain will make you grow. The point here is that manifesting all that you need in life comes at a cost. You must be prepared to pay the price and live your best life. And you've heard it more often than not - No pain? No gain! Right? It's a well-known fact. So, apply it in your life and live again.

Final Thoughts

Given the opportunity, there is no doubt that we would strive to live our best lives. We all want to achieve our dreams and find purpose in the life we live. But this never comes that easily. We often have to overcome challenges in our life path to get to where we want. In fact, we've been brought up with different notions surrounding our deepest desires. "Life is not easy," "money doesn't grow on trees," "hard work pays," and so on. With these perceptions, we go through life knowing that everything is all about overcoming challenges. Perhaps this negative mindset that we're brought up with alters how we view life and how we can manifest what we want.

The problem with the negative mindset that we've developed over time is that it drives us to reinforce the fears we have around our innermost desires. You want to manifest money, but it's easy to assume that money doesn't bring you happiness or that money doesn't come easily. So, you end up consoling yourself and finding proof of your negative perceptions about money. The worst thing that happens is that the universe listens to you through the vibrations you radiate.

The negative energy you radiate prevents you from staying aligned with what you want. Instead of focusing on what you want, you're focusing on what you don't want. The universe listens, and it vibrates through your energy frequencies. You're afraid of failing, and guess what happens? You fail in what you're doing. When you're afraid that you might never achieve your goals, the worst happens, and your goals seem far-fetched. That's how the universe works. Like attracts like, and you will always attract what you want into your life.

If you want to attract joy, bliss, abundance, money, fame, wealth, and love, etc., you need to focus on what you want. In other words, align yourself with what you really want to manifest into your life. Quit thinking of the worst that might happen. Change your narrative and start visualizing your best life. See yourself living your best life in the present moment.

This brings us to the importance of making the best out of the present moment you have in your life. You only have NOW to enjoy life and make things happen. The past is the past. Forget about what happened because you have no control over it. Similarly, the same case applies to your future. Stop worrying about the 'what ifs.' You can't exist in the future or the past and expect to enjoy life. Use meditation techniques to bring your mind to the present moment.

Learn to express gratitude for the things you have in your life. Before you start manifesting what you want, express gratitude. Be thankful that you're alive. Vibrate with positive energies about your life, and you will see your life transform. What you give is what you get. So, choose to radiate positive energies, and in turn, the universe will bring what you want into your life.

You now have all the tools you need to start manifesting what you want into your life. The first step is to ask the universe what you want. Be clear about it. You can't just say you want to make a lot of money. Be specific about it, and if possible, paint it on your vision board. Write it down how much you want. Asking is not as challenging as the second step of believing. Here, you need to believe with conviction that what you want will indeed manifest no matter how long it takes.

Perhaps, you may be worried because there is a lot going on in your life, and it's not easy for you to believe that you can attract what you want. You do not need to worry about how things will work out. The only thing you need to do is to BELIEVE. The same way you trust a true friend to always be there for you is the same belief you should have when trusting the universe to come through for you. Use the law of attraction. Practice it every day and make it a part of your life. The most successful people have proven it to work, so be sure that it will also work for you if you apply it the right way.

As you transition and align yourself with what you want to manifest, you need to remember that there will be conflicting energies to overcome. Yes, you want to attract something good into your life, but the mind will think otherwise. Your self-sabotaging behavior will affirm to you that you can't live the life of your dreams. The mind has a mind of its own, and it will drive you to think negatively even when you want to attract the best into your life. Accordingly, it's imperative that you learn how to silence your inner critic and live in the space where you believe in abundance, happiness, love, and the power of manifesting all that you want in life.

Are you ready to light up and live again? If your answer is yes, then you need to be prepared to pay the price. Living life fully demands that you get comfortable being uncomfortable. Pain is part of life, and you need to learn to live with it. Learn from your failures and do your best to grow through pain. Arguably, it is through difficulties that we become the best version of ourselves. You were born to live. So, do your best to manifest all that you want. Your current circumstances shouldn't stop you from moving forward. Just move into alignment and stay there.

Good luck!

If you enjoyed this book in anyway, an honest

References

Bible Hub. (2021). *Matthew 7:7 ask, and it will be given to you; seek, and you will find; knock, and the door will be opened to you*. Bible Hub: Search, Read, Study the Bible in Many Languages. https://biblehub.com/matthew/7-7.htm

Literary Devices. (2019, May 25). *A journey of a thousand miles begins with a single step*. https://literarydevices.net/a-journey-of-a-thousand-miles-begins-with-a-single-step/

www.ingramcontent.com/pod-product-compliance
Lightning Source LLC
Chambersburg PA
CBHW030917080526
44589CB00010B/352